The Radical Enlightenment

By
Yunfei Wang

Published by IISTE Publishing in the United States
ISBN-13: 978-1-62265-156-6

i

Contents

Preface

Writing is actually very hasty, because time is coming soon, and these messages must be quickly put into the world and completed.

But before this, there was a very long process of accumulation, which was part of the completion of my message, and this book is about which part of the foundation.

I need to put this part of the information into the world, participate in the construction of that big message, and continue to stir up my memory through feedback, and finally complete my message. There are a lot of messages behind, so I will tell you later.

This part of the message is not very large, but the amount of information inside is huge enough to shake the world.

Now it is at the crucial moment of role assignment. This kind of distribution has happened countless times in history, but every time it is distributed along the distortion. If this message is not intervened, it may be like that. Once heavy, there will be a lot of trouble.

So time is very urgent, and the message needs to be quickly spread to every corner of the world. These are the basic concepts. Everyone needs to know something, just like knowing our food and clothing.

From the East to the West, then from the West to the East, in the face of divinity, the message must talk to you through the boundaries of personality.

These messages are full of my twists and limitations, but they also tell you how to find the message.

When these messages are perceived in your life, please pass it on and tell your partner!

Chapter One: Message arrival

Come, the message has flowed into the world.Just as we saw the rising sun for the first time, although it has not yet seen it, its light has already filled the earth.We are still in the dark and do not know what it is, nor how it looks, but we can perceive the light and the sacred.The soul has long been illuminated by it, and you and I are waiting for a moment, and this moment is coming soon.

The sun is already in our sight, and all is about to begin.

This is the running process of a new structure, the creation of divinity.Don't refute me easily, because you are within limits, and also I am.

If I let me express it all in words, I can't do anything about it.Because these messages and concepts cannot be described.These messages seem to wake up to me, and I am recalled from my inner spirit. It is the original existence, but it is not perceived by us.

But I have to weave the language, to pass on these messages, and to complete the divine architecture.I can't resist it, but I can only finish that part of me.I don't know what the final accomplishment is, but I need to send a message to the world about how to wake up this dream.

The preparation in advance has been done, and the message has been laid for a long time. It is the white belly of the East.Divinity will reveal the truth at this moment, and humanity will return to the body of nature.

Although the seeds have already been planted, they have produced many distorted fruits. In the generations of human nature, they have not tasted the honey that God has made for us, but they are tasting the bitterness and ambiguity of twisting fruits and fruits.So cut off the twisted branches and go to the thick rattan.

This needs to awaken our inner, and what I rely on, language is the most unreliable thing, it is actually the shadow of the world, there is no good way, so I will pass the message in the name of the message, not The name of the language.I am not a person who will code words too much, and language is not my strength.

So don't read these languages in words.The language you read is just a covert.Please forget what I said, but remember what you feel.Your induction is communication with me, but the language is not.

My message and the message I want to convey are part of the world's divine architecture. I am integrated into this great creation and know what I am going to accomplish. It is my business and the responsibility of the gods.

This is a great creation, and I am also shocked by the great art of God.Only the greatness of integration into divinity can become great. This time, divinity will rise in human nature. I am waiting for such a moment, so I have to accomplish my business.The message of divinity has already flowed into the inner spirit of everyone. I will use some messages and concepts to arouse the inner divinity of each person and set the stage for the arrival of the gods.

The so-called gods are those who shine with the divine light.These people have established a channel of communication with the world that will bring us new knowledge.In fact, this is part of a huge structure. Humanity is only the soil where divinity is to be born. Now that the soil is fertile and can grow, the message will flow into the world through humanity.With the inflow of these messages, humanity will become part of the divine nature, blending with the divine nature.The gods are actually each of us. No one is special. Every life is for God.

These words sound a bit difficult to understand, it doesn't matter if I will start from the beginning.I am really not a good person to write. This task is a bit difficult for me.So I don't want to write complicated and lengthy, but use short words to quickly put the core message into the world.These messages will grow and will be constructed in many channels. The interpretation of these messages may be a lifetime, but now it is the basic structure.

The name of this book is called "The Radical Enlightenment" (Qi Yuan), which expresses revelation, Yuan means fundamental, and Qi Yuan means The Radical Enlightenment.This is also part of the construction of the whole message, and working for God is a glory for me.

The message is here, then we are ready to make a soul dialogue.

Chapter Two: Soul dialogue

This is a journey in which we are going to enter the realm of God, to understand the roots, and to complete ourselves.

The inherent limitations indicate that language is pale and weak in expression of divinity. Language is only the symbol of the message, not the message itself. The reason for all this will be mentioned in the discussion later, but now if we can't establish correct communication The way, then these messages will not be delivered.

What is going on is a soul dialogue, not a language dialogue.What we exchange is intrinsic experience, not language logic that floats on the surface.Don't understand these concepts at the language level, then you will be led astray by me.No matter how I filter it, it will distort the original concept. Language is the shadow of the world and needs to penetrate it.

So before you start, ask for your inner spirit, the self-defeating self that curls up within the flesh.It has long been bound by your seemingly powerful external twist with iron ropes.This time everything is unstoppable, and the message will go through all the shadows and talk to you.

This is a deeper exchange and is the inner consciousness of divinity.It is life for life, the soul for the soul.

No matter what kind of shell you wrap, no matter what kind of identity you are writing on these shells, what kind of knowledge is written, I will not say a word to them, the message will pass through the human self and reach the territory of your inner divinity. .

I am waking you up now, hoping that your eyes will not be reading while the soul is sleeping. Take all this into a new worldview.

Chapter Three: World view

The first obstacle that humanity faces before the world is how to treat it. This is a deep dilemma.

This seems to be a very difficult situation, because we don't know who we are facing.This seems to be a philosophical question, but in fact I don't understand philosophy.I have also tried to study philosophy, but those philosophies have been written for a long time. I feel that the inner hearts of those philosophers are not open enough to the world. How can they get the world with a closed heart? So I feel that their world is so complicated, and it seems that it is not clear.But here is not a philosophical question, because this is a message, part of the overall message architecture.The linguistic factors represented by the vocabulary of the world view will introduce people into a philosophical context, but now it is not to explore this context and its logic.Instead, the message to be released needs to start from here, because this is the part you can touch. This is just the vine that sticks out to you at the bottom of the valley. It is within your reach and then takes you out of the message. Some realms allow you to appreciate the whole world.

I will give you amazing answers, but your heart must be open. Everyone needs to find their own sense of the world. Now you are actually unaware of the world because there are some obstacles.Now the message is to penetrate these obstacles and bring you the world. The divinity will also be presented to the human nature in the original face. These things must be done before the mission of the gods.

I am very heavy because humanity is shackled by many inherent limitations. Opening this occlusion requires a strong desire to rise in your heart, a strong desire to touch the world.One thing to be aware of is that the external messages you receive are blinding your inner world, and each of us is naturally a shadow.This is a flaw in human nature, and later reading will let you know the reason for this flaw, but now you must be aware of it.Many years ago, I got this sentence in my heart. To know the world, first forget the world.Then the world was gradually forgotten by me, and some new concepts came to the surface.Recognizing that obstacles can get out of these obstacles, it is important to know that you are a shelter.

Start with cognitive limitations, then unfold all of the world, follow my message, and introduce the world.When everyone stands on the ground and feels the world, it will be guided by some feedback.We'll call it that is called "material" or "object" of things.what is that?In fact, you don't know, you are confirmed by the feedback of the message.Stone, land, river, air, sun, moon, planet, space, time, etc., everything.At this time you believe that you actually live among them, and I will believe in such a situation.The gentle wind, the wet rain, the solid earth, the wall that cannot pass through, will make you believe in the relationship between you and everything.Here is you and them, if you are observing, then they are your objective world.You will regard the sum of them and you as the whole of the world.Through your observations, the world is very large, and the universe is bigger than you and my imagination.It would be very reasonable to think of all of this as a whole.Science has strengthened this understanding by studying the relationship between things and things.I thought so a long time ago that this kind of understanding is inherent and natural.This is because you only accept the only channel of message feedback, the direct channel that the world feeds you back.The message you get on this direct channel, you will think it is a confirmed message, otherwise it is not.In this way, you have established a unique communication structure with the world. You cannot give up this structure. Giving up means that you have lost the truth of the world.For example, if you saw me, if I said that you didn't see me, then you would think that this is not true. I am lying is fake.But the real world is not like this. I am always between " in " and " out " . " In " is the result of the world's feedback to you, not my status.If I ask, you say that I am " in " , then where are I, you can't answer me, you can't confirm me in time and place.So the message for your direct channel feedback can't describe the world, it's just for you.

Now that you have found some problems, this world is not what you imagined before, nor what you feel, see, and confirm.Then return to that world view question, what is this world?What are we facing? How should we understand the world?Don't interpret this as a problem. This is not a problem. This is the message that the structure is unfolding for you. This is the arm you touch to the world.The relationship between them is not a question and an answer. The question does not correspond to the answer. The question is only to return us to the basic structure of the message, so that the consciousness of humanity returns to the inner of the message.This is part of the divine recovery, and the moment when human cognition is limited is the moment of divine recovery.

So I use the problem as a guide and point to the ontology of the world. When you realize that there is a problem in your world, then you are establishing a new communication channel with the world.There is a need for a worldview to guide this awareness and channel.What is the world's understanding of the structure of the message?

It is necessary to establish a new platform of consciousness so that human nature can have enough depth to understand the world, and there is enough deep humanity to construct divinity.In the process of my consciousness awakening, the world view was earlier realized, and even made a special summary. At that time, I called this world view concept.At that time, I was still thinking purely, but now I

8

need to integrate into the entire message structure as a message.

So what is concept theory, what is the world like in its eyes?Everything disappeared on this platform of consciousness without a trace, like matter, and these concepts disappeared without a trace.The world does not exist in the form of entities. The world perceived by human nature is not real. Those are not real beings (in fact, only fragments).The perception of the world is first broken!It may be painful, but there must be no other way to accept it.Mountains and rivers are not mountains and rivers, the ocean is not in the ocean, the sky is not in the sky, and the years are not in the years.The broken body can not be broken, the entity is actually your feeling, the consciousness of this physical world is fundamentally ideal.To understand the world as your measurement result, to regulate the world as a receptor, it sounds a bit absurd, all this is just because human nature is unconscious.

If it really disappears, what about the world?Has it disappeared yet?This is an important moment, when the external obstacles are removed, new consciousness will surface.The message will be introduced and the world will not disappear.It's just not what we used to understand.The core concept in concept theory is that the world is conceptual.Now we finally touched on the core concept of message construction, but the word concept is not very ideal, so you need to restore it into a message into your consciousness.Don't interpret this as a theory, but as a process of message construction. This time the process is done in human nature.This is a part of the construction of the whole world, and the whole world is also in the process of construction.And all this is built by the message, not the material we observe everyday.In the next chapter, Genesis, I will tell you how the world begins. At that time, your understanding of the message will be much deeper. Now plant the seeds of the worldview and finally grow an Eden.I have always emphasized that the world is a process of information construction, so the world can also be understood as a message.So what is the world in front of you?For example, an apple on a tree, is it not an apple?Is the earth not an earth?There is the whole universe, is it not the universe?No, there is no such thing.There is no one for your pre-existing apple, no one for your pre-existing earth, and no one for your pre-existing universe.Not a universe first, then you are in the middle of the universe.There is no such universe, which sounds very strange and does not meet the human experience.So what is this vast universe?There is no reason for it, and we feel it as the inner being of human nature, which seems to be unreasonable.So humanity is trapped in such a cage, and this universe that you think exists is only a frame of the world. It is not what you think in the vast consciousness of divinity.When the message takes you into trouble, you are closer to the truth.

I want to turn your mind through the message, penetrate the inherent obstacles, and let you see the back of the world.That is the divine nature hidden behind human nature.Now I want to give you an amazing answer. This answer is not the result of the answer. It is the channel through which your consciousness connects to the world.Listen, this universe is actually created for you.This is actually a universe that belongs to you. It can also be thought that you created this universe.You will not accept such a concept until now, you will ask me, is that apple just mine?Others will know to see the apple, the apple is clearly for everyone, not for me?I know this is your question.But that apple is only for you, not the apple for others.Why do I call this worldview conceptualism for a reason?The world is conceptual, the message, or the meaning itself, not the material itself.You are in confusion, I know.Now I tell you what the apple is and can be considered an agreement.It is the contract that you establish with the world, the commitment of divinity to you.It's just an agreement, just a promise. The reason why it is considered to be reality is because it is abiding by this agreement.When you touch that apple, it is not an entity, but the world and your agreement.This universe is also the agreement between the world and you. This agreement is strictly adhered to.The world only shows you the part you agreed with, while the others won't show it to you.Everything is also a contract. For your world or for your universe, it is just a contract between you and the world or the divinity. You only read the contents of this contract at your level of experience.

Understand that this contract is only signed with you. Everything you perceive is only valid for you. Your world is only your agreement with God and has nothing to do with other things.So don't think of your world, your contract as the whole world, it just corresponds to you.For example, the apple, the apple is just your apple, the other thing is not your apple, I know, this does not meet your experience.Understand this, if there is a single apple, then this apple is the only one, if Apple is the only one, then Apple is absolutely the same, if Apple is absolutely the same, then Apple only has a unique state, if Apple exists unique State, then you see the apple, others will not see the apple.Because Apple's state is unique, it can't exist in two different fields of view at the same time.This is not in line with your experience, so Apple is not the only existence of independence. Since Apple shows different states, such as the appearance of each person's eyes, then each state of its state is different, since it is not the same, then each state It corresponds to an apple.And each state is the contract between the world and the owner.The world is unfolding for you, not the world itself, and you are playing inside.You will only see your apple and never see someone else's apple.

So why do you all see a similar apple, which will determine how the divinity establishes a contract with you, how the contract was built, and this will be one of the tasks of the gods.This task is huge and arduous, but it is also exciting.What I am talking about is not simply referring to your personality, because your personality is also based on a huge contract. Your consciousness-awareness mechanism is very old, just like the atoms in your body.You see something similar to others, like the apple, because you are all built on a similar contract.

In such a worldview, the meaning of the physical entity disappears and is replaced by the meaning of the concept.Everything is the result of some contract, not independent.The world is not an independent existence in the process of construction.So every personality is a participant in the construction of the world, and can also be understood as the creator of the world. This concept is very important. What kind of world you want to build, what kind of world the world gives you.Many times the world gives you the right to choose, but you don't know how to choose.Because the limitations of distortion are ubiquitous, you are observing the world. Just like you think of an independent apple, what you want is not what divinity wants. Humanity does not understand the meaning and correspondence of construction. You must be big. The bias will be small. If you want to be good, it will be bad. If you want life to be partial, it will be death. If you want to get the bias, you will lose it. You will say to God, I want what you don't give me, God will answer, this is what you want.Because human nature does not recognize divinity and is not integrated with divinity, you do not know what you want to represent in the divine world, because you do not understand divinity and do not understand the process of world construction.

This is a very deep question. There will be a special chapter discussion. Now I have outlined a world view. This world view is based on the concept. With such a basic understanding, I will provide the next chapter, Genesis. The basis of the message, under this basic world view, open this most important chapter.

Chapter Four: Genesis

Finally, to open this important chapter, many core concepts will be revealed in this chapter, you will understand the beginning of the world and the roots of divinity.But I must admit that I describe the world and the divinity from the perspective of human nature. This is my essential limitation.I can't get rid of the distortions that the personality itself brings.So this is still not a theory or a certain standard. I am not telling you what the world or divinity looks like. It will look like this. But this way is distorted by me. My message must also pass my limitations. Accepting and sending, I can't stand at the fundamental height of the divine to verify the world, and no one can do it. Personality can only do what personality can do.

So still don't understand these messages as answers, this is not the answer.This is only part of the construction of the message, and it is the part that has been distorted through my personality. As for what it is, I want to say, I don't know.Those " fundamentals " need to be accomplished through the power of the gods are the tasks of the gods.I am just doing what I have to do during the construction of the message.

The screening of these messages is a matter for the gods. Now I want to send out these messages to show you the world.

(1) The first day

What happened to the first day of the world?The world has begun.Is the Almighty God completing this mission?No, the world cannot be called the world on this day, and God cannot be called God.At this time the world is very quiet and very quiet.So what is this world at this time?He is not, is not there, is no.So very quiet.You may not understand everything at this time, but I can't understand it.Because there is no understanding at this time, nothing is done.This is the first day. It is actually a wrong name, because it was not even on the first day, but it was the earliest. We called him the first day.There was nothing on that day, nothing.

Although there is nothing, everything starts here.Now we can't understand this thing, but we must understand such a thing. If we want to understand the world, some concepts need to be introduced from the first day, how to understand no, no existence, no such state, no way to understand, Because there is nothing.Now a concept comes to help you understand this non-existent state.This concept is the "infinity."Then no, no, no, what is it?It is because of infinity.But this infinite concept is easily confused with our everyday infinite concepts, so it must be clarified that the infinite concept of humanity comes from a sense of extension, such as the concept of straight lines.In fact, this is a distorted understanding of the concept of infinity. From the perspective of the world, there is no such infinite extension. This understanding comes from the confusion of the concept of finiteness and infinity. It is a finite infinity, and it has unlimited finiteness. The two concepts are not combined in this way, so they must be distinguished.

So what is " infinity " ?How to understand?It is not to give you a definition of the same thing, but to integrate into the inner spiritual understanding of human nature through the message.Infinity means no limit.Why do you think that a thing exists? That is because this thing has been restricted. Through the world view, you will be told that this thing has signed many contracts with the divine.Apple has become Apple because it has been limited, it is limited.So you know them, but there is no, no existence, no such state, no restrictions, no contract, you can't find it, it is no, no, no.What is important here is the understanding of infinity, that is, there is no limit.Not a limited thing extends infinitely.

On this day, I know that the world at this time is no, there is no or no.I also know that it is actually a manifestation of infinity, then this day is over.In the later words, I unified no, no or no, no.Ok, everything is going to start now.

(2) The beginning

First of all, quiet your soul, first understand the " infiniteness " of experience , what kind of situation is that. ""Infinity " is unlimited , it does not exist. ""Infinity " means an absolute no, it has nothing to do with everything, no connection, no agreement.Because of this, everything did not begin, but it was born in its inner.These are not words that can be expressed by the language. Now it is the dialogue of the soul. I use the inner spirit to understand this situation. At this time, there is nothing, and there is nothing. However, nothing is not lonely. It still has attributes that are " infinite. " .But such expression is wrong again. There is no such thing as " infinity " .This seems very contradictory. Since there is nothing, how can there be such an attribute as " infinity " ?The things at that time were actually incomprehensible, because the principles at that time were not maintained with understanding.It can only be said that we can see it roughly. There is no attribute of " infinity " , but this attribute is negated. It is described in a contradictory language. It can be said that non-existence is " infinite " , but without this attribute, Exist but denied.

With all sorts of doubts, we finally came to this moment.

This is how the creation of the world, causes divine where is all this just because something happened, that is a question and there is no asked a question, "Who I am."This is the fundamental question of divinity, and this world has broken out.So simple, the world has started so.Who can think of this is because of a problem.Our vast world is actually because of a problem.Think of the world view I told you, why is it conceptualism, because the world begins with a problem, and everything is built around this problem, which is the essence.This is a great question, and divinity begins. Before this question, everything is fine. After this question, all problems exist.In the following chapters, I will give an answer to the divinity. Deity is not our so-called all-powerful God concept. If you want to understand the question about divinity, then wait for the birth of this world. Then I am telling you what divinity is. ?

Seemingly so simple beginning, such a simple question, was actually the most difficult problem, this great question, directly spawned the birth of the "three bases" of the. "Three basic "building the foundation of the world, as the fundamental constitution of the world.

(3) Three basics

I have been aware of the " three basics " for more than ten years, but I have always concealed my heart. I have never revealed a little bit of information. Because it is too important, I can't rashly spread these messages to those who know the truth.Now I want to take it out and give it to the process of constructing this message to complete the process of constructing this message.

" Three basics " refers to the three basic properties of this world.These three basic properties are non-existence, designation and exploratory.

How are the " three basics " selected, and what are they going to do ?Everything comes from that basic question.

There is no denial of everything, but it is not a stable structure, because there is nothing at that time. Negative points can only point to the non-existent self. When negation points to itself, even if there is no existence, you have to ask, what is not there. ?This question makes the non-existence point to it. This point is the root of the world's outbreak and the root of the beginning of divinity.

When this point occurs in the absence of a body, there is no existing attribute, which can be called non-existence.Non-existence is no longer empty, but is not directed. Non-existence and non-existence are different states of one thing. Non-existence is pointed by itself, and non-existence is purely empty.

Through that negative structure, the world has its first nature and no existence.

But non-existence is still a negative structure. At this time, there is only one thing in the world that is non-existent. When negating the direction derived from the structure and pointing toward non-existence, another nature is born. Non-existence can be understood. to "infinity", then "infinity" is a negative point itself, i.e., defining "infinity" of.The second property represents the nature of the point, the designation.

This is equivalent to what the "infinity" to be asked, and that is "infinity" is "Yes."It is limited to "unlimited sex".This limit is specified.

The basic description of the world can be expressed as follows: the world is the result of non-existence being designated.

The definition of " infinity " is the basic contradiction of the existence of the world.

Why is this thousand worlds born? Because this contradiction has unlimited solutions, it can create unlimited possibilities.

The two basic properties of non-existence and designation are collisions and norms of infinity and finiteness.It is a compromise of two natures that cannot be compromised. In this process of coordination, a third basic nature is explored.

Exploratory representation of the process of nonexistence and specified compromises, which is done in a collaborative manner.Exploratoryly demonstrate that the solution to the existence of this world is precisely the way of solution, which is the basis of world prosperity.The world we exist is one of the outcomes of a compromise, one chosen in an infinite scheme.

Maybe my language is not clear enough, then describe this process again :

There is no existence (negative) → and the negation at this time can only point to the non-existent negation (negative negation) → the negated negation is non-existence (negative negation is denied, non-existent property is established) → does not exist Sex is represented (no existence is described as non-existence) → described by non-existent attributes (because non-existence at this time represents non-existence, so non-existent attribute description does not exist, described as, negation Sexuality and Infinity)→ The nonexistence of property paradox (negation of nothing can only point to itself, negation to negation, here we need to emphasize an important issue, that is, negation of negation equals affirmation of this proposition, pay attention to negation at this time Negation does not mean affirmation, because negation cannot be affirmatively negated. At this time, negation means infinity, and infinity cannot be affirmed. This proposition does not hold.The so-called negative pointing negation only indicates the existence of directivity, and the negation is always directed. → The designation is established (this is one of the key properties of the world establishment, and its basic principle is that the non-existent negative attribute refers to the self-referential, and Throughout the construction of the entire world.)→ Specificity-specific triggering (when the specifiedness points to non-existence, the non-existent negative attribute denies this direction, that is, when the designation does not exist, the non-existence will deny this identification, expression This identification is not a nonexistence of identification.This triggers the limitations specified properties.This principle is very important, and this is the basic principle of existence.It refers to any qualitative point are non-non-existent.)→ Specified sexually specified triggers (when everything points to the wrong, the specified sexuality is triggered to the specified, that is, the specifiedness is in the direction of non-existence, the specified property is pointing to the non-existent attribute, but the specified property Pointing is not all attributes that are not existential, so this is a completed process, not a result.This ending triggers an exploratory) → exploratory establishment (the world will construct a process of exploration with a pointing and pointing negation to complete a world process) → world construction.

So far the basic world has been built.

But just as designation can never behave as nonexistence, language can't express nonexistence as well.Rely on to express the initial description of the world is impossible, which refers to qualitative limitations, I can only tell you part, while the other part will be missing forever, that's it.

Through my description, you may have seen the image of a horse, but this horse is partially obscured. You may see a white horse, but if it is not covered, it may be a zebra.

But no matter what, now we still have an image, although that is not all, but still through some plots, see the world and not see it.

(4) Creation continues

The basic structure of Genesis is completed, but this is not a stable structure, not a constant world. On the contrary, the world is destined to be unconventional. The world will be developed in such a form. This is the problem faced by the divine.I describe the process of creating the world in an objective way. It seems to watch a movie that has nothing to do with us. We are also participants in this event, so we must return to subjective understanding of divinity. There will be a special chapter. Describe the destiny in the divine world, that is something related to us.But before those begin, what is to be opened is the story of the creation of the universe and a picture.The foundation already exists, the creation will continue, how the universe was created, how the stories of the world are written, and then come with my message.

Chapter Five: Cosmic creation

(1) The basic concept

Before talking about the creation of the universe, we need to change some distortions and establish a channel for the construction of the message.

Now we need to change the concept of " correct " . People want to find a correct way to solve the problem, but " correct " does not apply to the world itself, nor to the moment when the universe is created. "" Correct " only exists in the scope covered by the designation, and cannot cover the world itself as a description.The world does not originate from a certain right thing, but originates from a " error " . This " error " is a contradiction that cannot be specified and cannot be resolved.

Therefore, the world does not operate in a specified way, and its model is a process of discussion.There is no powerful theory that can determine everything in the world or the universe.What we need to understand is the way the world is explored.

The laws of physics do not represent such a profound concept of the world, but represent the result of a discussion.The reality world we are facing is actually one of the results of this world.This result and the world are not a concept.

So the universe I describe in the message, and the universe in your heart may not be one thing.Your inner concept of the universe is just the real universe. It is a universe full of space, time and stars, and the law of the universe that you discovered.

20

The worldview has been changed before, and now it is necessary to use this worldview to change the concept of reality into a description of meaning.

In the universe I want to describe, there are no spaces, time, stars, and those laws.The message I want to convey is a basic contradiction. What the world wants to be, depends on your observations.

For the world our message comes from the back of it, the world after observation and performance has been established, it is only a result.Through the concept of these messages, the concept of the universe has been established one-sidedly.This concept actually has a profound impact, and it also hinders the way the message is constructed, and some distortions have occurred.

Such a cosmological concept stems from the description within the specified nature and is a world of observers.Now you need to leave such a world, so you want to understand the world and forget about the world first.

In fact, we asked the wrong question. We have been asking, what is this universe?And there is no such problem in this world, and the universe cannot be described by " yes " .The universe is nothing. "It is a worldwide problem "is only a problem within the prescriptive, instead of one.Designation expresses the limitation of infinity, which is characterized by limitations and is a finite expression.

So we can't ask this question because the universe is not a identifiable state, but a state in confirmation.

What needs to be established is the basic contradiction and the state of designation. This is the way the message is constructed and the state of construction.

The result of the universe is that the basic contradictions correspond to the results of the designation.Or the universe of the appearance corresponds to the observer.It is the surface specified for the observer.

Do you understand this truth? Generally speaking, your universe is only for you.Your universe is the description of the identification that corresponds to your observations.So when you face your universe and ask what it is, you are faced with a universe that is limited by a given nature.When you face the conclusions of your universe, it has nothing to do with the fundamental universe.You only exist in the form, and your conclusions only exist in the form.You ask " what is " in the form , and just ask what the table is " what " .

It is now necessary to establish a basic contradiction and a specific relationship to establish the essence of the universe.

In the last chapter, we learned about the three basics, but the three basics are the basic nature of the world, but they are not the basic contradictions of the world.Even if there is a tribasic nature, the universe may not be created, because the nature itself is only the nature itself.There are limitations to the description, I can only describe yes or no, but it is neither.The basic contradiction is not a three-base nature, but the basic contradiction is a three-base nature.

I am also troubled. The world is always in two aspects of contradiction. This also requires me to use contradictory expressions.This is because human nature itself is in the limits and is part of the specific meaning.So what is needed is a soul dialogue, not a logical one.

Need to leave some of the inherent patterns that designation brings to us.Because we are facing the world this time.This is a much larger concept than we have understood before.Cognition will change once, limitations will be recognized, and even human behavioral rules will change.Through the basic concept, it will be extended to all aspects of human nature, which will be reflected in the following chapters.

Now let's complete the message about the creation of the universe and enter our understanding in a certain way.

22

(2) The specified limitations

Designation is the key property of participating in the creation of the universe. We learned this nature in Genesis, and it is one of the three basics.It is expressed by the non-existent negation structure self-pointing.

Because the designation points to non-existence, but non-existence has negative attributes, which means infinity, neither undefined nor negated as a limit.

Faced with such a pointing object, the designation is faced with limitations and can only express a limited affirmation of infinity.Designation is characterized by finiteness.The creation of the world can be described as the result of a limited description of infinity.

This directional limitation is very important, it is the fundamental reason for the creation of the world.It is this limitation that brings us the universe and the foundation of the real world.If the stipulation can point to all the nature of non-existence, then everything will not happen later.Because the world has no space to explore.

The specification limit can be understood in this way. When the specified property points to A , B and A do not match.

(3) The unique directivity of the specified

A very contradictory concept, the limitations of designation determine the meaning of not being able to point to nonexistence.But non-existence is the only point of designation.That is to say, the designation cannot point to the whole of nonexistence, and the designation points to all of the nonexistence.

The only point of specification is that there is no existence, and there are no other options.Designation covers all meanings of nonexistence and is a complete point.Designation is not meant to point to a part of nonexistence but to all.

Non-existent attributes are simple and unique. When there is no existence and no point, non-existence is unique.There is no point, that is, when we don't describe, don't express, don't explore, nonexistence is just nonexistence.But once it is pointed at it, its negative attribute will negate everything, and all directions cannot express nonexistence.

Very strange, no pointing will not be separated, a point will be separated.

But the designation is to point to non-existence, to point to all the meanings it produces.Therefore, even if the pointing meaning is separated by the non-existent negative attribute, the separated part is still pointed to by the designation, thereby indicating the unique directivity of the designation.

(4) The basic contradiction

The non-existent negative attribute, the limitation of the designation and the unique directivity of the designation lay the foundation for establishing the basic contradiction of the world.This condition is not a direct factor in the creation of the universe.The basic condition corresponds to the attribute, not the process of creation.

These conditions and attributes are in place, and the creation of the universe will begin.

This confusing world is the result of entanglement by three conditions that build the basic contradictions of the universe.

These three conditions are triggered by the non-existence of the pointing. When the specified property points to the non-existence, the specified property is expressed as a limited part and at the same time exhibits another negative part because of the non-existent negative attribute.

Now point the pointer to C. When the specification points to C , then the nonexistence is represented as C , and the nonexistence is denoted as C as a locality attribute.C exhibits non-existence attributes and has limited attributes.

The expression for C can be expressed as nothing for everything.

If you use some common sense to understand, you can roughly understand it as infinitesimal.It's just that it's not infinitely small, you can't use ordinary mathematical concepts. This is a construction concept. The so-called expression is just a general description for the needs of understanding.

How to understand that for everything without such a description, when the specified sex points to non-existence, the non-existence is still non-existent, but this non-existence is characterized by a directional attribute.So C is none, but it is nothing for everything, so it is described by finiteness.

It is necessary to clarify a message that is limited.Don't interpret finiteness as a thing, to define a scope for something, or to understand it as a boundary.The finiteness indicates the description and the attribute bearer, and does not necessarily specify the scope.This is the limitation of language, so don't look at what I said, but focus on my language.

When the designated points of C is, the absence of a negative structure immediately denied this point, C may be regarded as the absence of, but not the absence of C.Once C is pointed, another condition is available at the same time.It represents a negation of the nonexistence of the C description.

We express this part of the negative meaning as Cp .For Cp it can be stated that everything is nothing for it.

Cp represents a negation of a specified orientation.For the description of finiteness, Cp is infinitely possible.

From the understanding of our common sense, Cp can be understood as infinite.But Cp can't be understood as infinity in mathematical concepts. Cp is not a big one in the comparative sense, but a constructive concept, which means negation of pointing.But from the perspective of personality consciousness, it seems to describe some big concept.

Cp means negating the designation as none, but does not emphasize how it is done. It is just a concept and condition.It is also a trend, it is to do so.However, Cp did not do it. If it is done, the world will be completed.

Because the designation points to all of the nonexistence, when the concept of Cp is derived, it will also be pointed to by the specification.Other concepts will be derived. This is a process of discussion. The world is in a construction and has not been completed.

It is such a process of exploration that creates opportunities for the complex world of creation.

In the process of creating this opportunity specified in point is a cross-cutting nature of the participants, we can now put to the specified representations as I.

Everything is the result of C , Cp and I.These three conditions constitute the basic contradiction of the universe.

Both C and Cp can be considered as descriptions of nonexistence, C is a non-existent specified field of view, and Cp is a negative field of view of nonexistence.Due to the participation of I , the nonexistence is distinguished.But you can't think that nonexistence is divided into two. C and Cp refer to one thing, that is, nonexistence.C and Cp are one thing and not two things.So C and Cp are highly correlated because they are one.This is a very contradictory concept that cannot be understood in the limited vision, but the world will not conform to the correct concept in the limited vision, but will reflect contradictions in the limited vision.

So for our limited vision, we can only express it with a contradiction, that is, C and Cp are one but two.

This is the mystery of nature. It is not done by the so-called correctness within the scope of the concept of designation.

I think of the description of the world in Lao Tzu's Tao Te Ching, life, two, two, three, three things, in fact, this description is very covered, if the hard process of this creation process may be somewhat far-fetched.But substituting wish to explain, there is no representation as it can not be called one, one should specify the nature I, when prescriptive point, generate C, then was I with C, expressed in two.When I points to C , Cp is generated , which is I , C and Cp , which is expressed as three.The basic contradictions brought about by these three concepts produce everything.

These concepts have been in my mind for more than a decade, and the scenes were still vaguely remembered. They were still very young, and they were thinking about how to create these problems.I remember that time, walking on the street, thinking about these problems, I thought of two things, one is zero relative to everything, and the other is zero relative to everything.Suddenly found that these two things do not exist in this world, if they do not have these two things then they do not exist?This shows that it does not exist, it is the original revelation.Following this revelation, the world is gradually becoming clearer.

(5) The beginning of the universe

The basic contradiction exists, then the universe exists, no.The universe is not a basic contradiction. Even if basic contradictions exist, the universe does not exist.

The basic contradiction expresses all possibilities and does not express everything.Basic contradictions create endless possibilities and structures, but they are not selected.

The basic contradiction expresses the possibility, this is a basic category, but all possibilities are not the universe. It is said in the worldview that the universe is a description of the observer.That is to say, the expression of basic contradiction is only to express the possibility, and it does not solve the problem of who is expressed.And the universe is for whom to express it, and to whom it is expressed.

The basic answer to the beginning of the universe is to express to whom.There is no such universe, only after it is expressed to the observer, the universe is there for the observer.I don't know if you understand this meaning?

The universe is a description of the basic contradiction that the observer constructs.

The universe is for the observer, not the world. The universe is also confined. It only expresses part of the meaning of the basic contradiction rather than the whole meaning.There is no universe that is there and we are in the middle of the universe.

The universe is a collection of all the points of the observer, a contract between you and God.

The universe expresses the basic contradiction in creating a description for you.

The universe does not begin with basic contradictions but begins with observers.

(6) The first observation

One day, the sky was blue, and I looked out the window through the window and saw a very clear view in the distance.At this time, I suddenly asked myself a deep question. Whose vision is this vision in my eyes?I am also waiting for the answers of the gods.

My vision is already large enough, but it is still not the first observer, who made the first observation of the world and made the world construct it.

This question relates to the way the world is done. In fact, this is not my task, but the task of the gods.

But I am obligated to ask this question, which is also part of the construction of the message.

In fact, I can't interfere too much with the thinking of the gods. The confirmation of the first observer is the choice of the way the world is done.It may be a point of specificity, perhaps a more complex relationship.

But no matter what, the first to observe the world is the eye of God, the recovery of divine wisdom.From that moment on, God woke up and it was going to complete its masterpiece.The world has unimagined levels that go far beyond the universe we understand.

(7) leaving a suspense for a picture

There will be a chapter devoted to a picture, which can represent the process of creating the world.There is also a legendary process that this picture gets.

Chapter Six: Creation enlightenment

This chapter should actually belong to the tasks of the gods. This is to explore some of the attributes and meanings that the world has shown in the process of discussion.

This part of the work is very arduous and huge, and it is not a problem that I can solve under the limit of my people.

The message of this part is very broken, God's way of creation has not yet been known, and now these broken messages can only be expressed as apocalyptic words.

So this is still not a theory or a conclusion, nor a result of confirmation. These can only be seen as a message that has been distorted by me, and it is my revelation of the tasks of the gods.

There are some amazing conclusions, because I am watching you from the other side of the world.

(1) My way of thinking

In fact, I have been entangled in the way I think, and that can't even be called an ideal way.But this way of thinking can bring efficiency to me.

I feel that a lot of messages are remembered by me, not what I found.Because my thinking is not based on logic, I almost gave up the concept of common sense in my teenage years, and my thinking is not based on basic common sense.Then I summed up this situation, that is, to know the world, first forget the world.I have done this forgotten process very early, and of course there is a price, that is, my school seems to be in a mess.When the world is forgotten, it is actually through a layer of barriers that can be touched with the underlying messages.

A lot of chaotic messages are constantly input into the mind, and even the relationship is not clear, but there will be a moment when some concepts are suddenly detected, and the chaotic messages are suddenly unified by a certain vision.

It seems to be chaotic, but it has super high efficiency. If you are in a certain limitation, some meaning will never be obtained.It's not these meanings you don't know, but you don't have the opportunity to recall them, and I created such an opportunity.

Many times you are obsessed with the right, but you are disgusted with the mistakes, but the correctness can only be expressed under the limited conditions. The correct obsession is the fascination of limitations.Just as the designation is finally denied, the correctness will also be denied.The world begins with a mistake because it acknowledges it but denies it.

(2) the binary phase of C and Cp

One of the two is a very cumbersome statement. Under any limited conditions, this meaning cannot be understood as correct, because any direction will trigger negation, but the error is correct.So don't try to understand this conclusion as correct. What needs to be studied is how it is discussed under specified conditions.

C and Cp are two of one thing.They all represent nonexistence, no representation of the second nonexistence, and no second nonexistence.Their distinction is a different description of the designation, that is, they form a meaning for the observer, different observers will get different conclusions about them, see different worlds.

This shows that this complex world level is not a pure world. You cannot understand the world from a simple perspective.You are just in a field of vision, how do you understand things in other fields of vision.Only return to the basic contradiction, where the center can lead to other horizons.

31

Regarding the binary phase of C and Cp , I can't say it clearly, but I can't express it, but do you understand it?Do you understand the thing I said unclear?I can understand the thing that I don't know.Because you are an experienced person, you will know.

(3) Needs to establish effective tools

This is the mission of the gods, and there is still a distance from this goal.Now is the beginning stage, and the information construction is not enough.Lack of tools can make a lot of work intensive, and only stay on the surface.

(4) The construction and nature of basic substances

This discussion is a long time after the creation of the world, so there is a fault of understanding, but this is the message that I have emerged, perhaps part of the big message building.But there must also be a part of my distortion here, just to provide information for the mission of the gods.

When the designation points to non-existence, the non-existence of the pointing is expressed as C , and the non-existent negative structure is expressed as Cp .At this time, it will be found that when the specification points to C , the meaning of Cp is diverged.Cp is now infinitely possible.

But Cp is also pointed to by designation, because designation points to all meanings of nonexistence.When Cp is pointed, Cp now behaves as C , but it also fires a Cp , so that C is actually pointed to eternity, and Cp changes its form because of pointing.

Therefore, the material form needs to be divided into two categories, the C state and the Cp state.I also call it the stator and the mover.The stator does not move and the mover changes.Since C is eternally pointed, C does not change, but since C is a description for Cp within its direction, C does not change but has a structure.So C is more like a recorder, recording the description of Cp .

The C state and the Cp state are two phases of one element of a substance, or two elements are described by two phases.The C state or Cp state cannot be described independently .In common sense we may have split these two states.

If for the physical form of the real world, the C state is like a photon, and the Cp is like a proton electron.

When the Cp state is pointed, it can be understood as a change of description. Corresponding to the real world, it can be understood as a change in the state of proton electrons. When this change occurs, the Cp state is pointed to become a C state. At the same time, the C state is specified to trigger another Cp state.

On the surface is a Cp A move from state to B, the state has changed, in fact, starting from the basic contradiction in the world of such a thing did not happen, ACp is ACp, BCp is BCp, is two states, is not a state Moved the location.There is no moving position, it is two states.

But why do we think that just a Cp state moves the position, it does not change other things just changes the position, it is because the C state is pointing to the direction forever and exciting another Cp state, the message is Stay intact.In this process, the Cp state becomes the C state, and then the C state is excited by another Cp state. This is the completion of a message.

As the message is maintained, only a specific change has occurred.So it will give people the feeling that the Cp state has not changed, but it has changed in one aspect.

Therefore, photon substances are excited when the state of proton electrons changes.

The C state is always pointed, and it will tell you a problem. The C state keeps the material information stable, and it remains unchanged.

Our vision is actually the Cp state of view, because we can see the light, remember that this is an incomplete vision, you are in the Cp state, you can not observe the world.What you see is just a projection of the Cp state, which is the projection world given to you by the transcription of the C state.This projection is just a fragment of the world that corresponds to the level pointed to by a Cp state.

The best viewing angle is in the C state, because C specifies the C- state, which is pointing one direction forever and C can contain all the information of the world.

If you look at the world in photons, you will see the whole world.

Due to the constant pointing of the C state, we are told that the state of the C state is unchanged.The C state changes the message without changing the state.Corresponding to the real world, in fact, that speed of light does not change.

However, the state of the C state does not mean that the speed of light does not change.The constant speed of light is an observation of the Cp state of view, and the C state is unchanged from the basic contradiction of the world.These two are actually not a problem, but the speed of light is a problem that is triggered by the state of the C state.Corresponding to photons is not a pure C state, but a Cp state, because photons are described in the Cp state.The constant C state does not correspond to the speed of light, not the speed, but the meaning or direction is constant.Speed is a description of the Cp state.But when the Cp state changes, the description of the speed of light changes, and the speed value changes.However, the specified orientation does not change, that is, even if the speed of light changes in the description of the specified nature, it is a state transformation process, which will be described as continuous.

If the C state is constant, then why do we see that the particle photons it represents are moving, just the opposite is that the photons are not moving, and the photons are in a static state.The movement of photons is because you are in the field of view of Cp .It is the Cp state that is moving, not the photon.The movement of photons is described in Cp , while Cp describes the state change.It is the Cp state rather than the photon that moves at the speed of light .The speed of light is the speed of the Cp state rather than the speed of the photon.

This is the material property represented by the one state with two phases.

(5) The explanation of particles and forces

It is known by our common sense that this real world is made up of elementary particles, so what is the elementary particle?Why do you generate elementary particles?

This is an interesting question, and what is the role of the basic particles.This is a divine problem. I can't say that I know. I can only pass the message that I understand. There are also my distortions in these messages.

The construction of the added message, even if there is distortion, there is a mechanism to cancel the sale.

So what is the basic particle?Simply put, the elementary particle is the Cp junction.What is the role of force?Simply put, force is the untie of Cp knots.

It can only be simple, and the complexity is the task of the gods.This is the basic revelation, so it is an overview.

What is the cause of all this? Everything starts from the basic contradiction. When the designation points to non-existence, it is pointed to be described as C and negatively motivated into Cp .That is to say, the designation of the C to the C causes the meaning of Cp to diverge.

But Cp is still pointed to by specifying, when Cp becomes C and C inspires Cp .Now I found a problem, which is equivalent to a Cp over C hit a knot.This knot can actually be seen as a basic particle.The actual problem will be more complicated than what I described, but it is roughly the case.From the state of Cp , various forms of the knot can be derived.These forms show the morphology of the elementary particles.But these knots are for some kind of observation. It is this observer who seems to have a knot in this place, because the real world is in this kind of observation, so the particles are discovered by us.

When the state of Cp is described, Cp is in the structure of a certain knot. When Cp is pointed to indicate a state change , there is a process of untangling between the states of the differentiated Cp . The process of the untie is force. .

The shape of the knot determines the form of force. There are only two kinds of forces. One is exclusion and the other is attraction.Corresponding to the two forms of the knot, one is open knot and the other is closed.How to understand the relationship between knot and force, you can use a metaphor, when the meaning of Cp diverges, you can think of it as a rope stretched to the two ends, this state can be understood as open knot, showing outward rejection.However, if a knot is made in the middle of the rope and the two ends are stretched as hard, then it will shrink within the knot. This state can be understood as a closed knot, which is expressed as attraction.

Like gravitation, we are in a closed state. This may be Cp divergence. The basic knot described is a closed knot for all Cp states. It is characterized by attraction.

There may be more types of forces than we think, but there are only two outcomes.The structure of the knot of a particle can be very complicated. Like a Chinese knot, the way of knotting may be different, and the type of force will be different.

(6) Extreme destruction and exploration

This is also one of the important contents.This involves an important issue, which is the specified description of the designation.Whether this designation is explicit when the specifier points to a concept.The designation requires a clear expression, but the designation cannot be expressed.Because it points to non-existence, it is a negative structure.Designation cannot be determined by nonexistence, but designation is the identification.This is a contradiction, so a process of discussion will begin.

There are some ambiguities in it, so there is no clear boundary for specifying the designation. This is a discussion structure, which corresponds to the description produced by the description.

The ambiguity of the boundaries has created a gap in the world, and these gaps are the gateway to all worlds.

With regard to the direction of designation, it is necessary to use a contradictory language description, which is a clear ambiguity.Very contradictory, but true.The level we understand is within a limited scope. The scope of this limitation does not correspond to the world, so the contradiction we get is not contradictory to the world itself, but it is.

This unclear gap in a clear context has brought many opportunities to the world.

With our sense of touch, it feels like a clear world. The state of matter is clearly distinguished, large, small, long, short, fast, slow, and of various colors.But these are not the essence of the world, the world is very vague in nature, but the designation will give a specific meaning to the specified state.The world describes the observers, not the world itself.The world is describing the meaning of being effective for the observer, so your clarity is the validity of your creation, the contract between you and God.

So you won't confirm any state, what is this state?Without this problem, only you have a relationship with it.

This kind of identification is unclear and how to establish a discussion. There is still a lack of information in it, but now we ignore many of the problems and explore the problem of extinction.

When specifying nonexistence of directivity, produced Cp, Cp represents a possible infinite.Cp will also be pointed to by specificity, but the point of specifying can't specify infinite possibilities. The specification is in the direction of Cp , and a vague coverage description is made.This is another task that cannot be completed. There are too many clear and unclear questions.

Because there is no basic tool, the description is very vague, so it can only be understood in my description.

It is necessary to describe a process that causes the meaning of Cp to diverge when the designation points to non-existence .Now use an image instead of speed.At this time, it can be understood that the speed is infinitely fast.When C is pointed, Cp dissipates its meaning at an infinitely fast rate, and the meaning of Cp is widespread in the world.At this time Cp is pointed, Cp can't describe the world in an infinitely fast sense, and the specifiedness points to a certain category.But Cp is not a category, but an infinite possibility.The result specification specifies Cp in a specific way .

This form of description may be understood as the expansion of meaning.That is to say , the description of Cp is completed by the expansion of meaning .I don't know if I can understand this. I can understand it. I can't describe Cp , but I can describe it all the time.But this description must be in a specific pattern.

There is a lot of information missing here. Now I understand that our world is expanding, like the big bang.But it is not exactly the case.This expansion is not in the sense of volumetric speed, but should be understood as the expansion of the description and the expansion of meaning.

So how fast is this expansion, which can be measured by the stator, because the relative world of C is described as static, so the expansion speed can be seen by the stator describing C.Because photons are stators, the speed of vacuum is the speed at which the world expands.

This expansion of the meaning of the world is pointed by the designation, so this meaning is constant.But this is not the reason for the constant speed of light. The specification refers to the speed of meaning rather than pointing, and the speed of light is not constant.

As the description grows, the speed of light is getting smaller.The initial speed of light was fast, but it quickly became smaller.

Designation now actually specifies a big world, but describes a small world.There is a lot of ambiguity between them, and there are many potential meanings in the world.

Extreme extinction exists in these vague senses. This is a sphere, which is equivalent to the world (because the world is described, our universe is coordinated into a field of vision) , and we will find that any two large rings that describe the same will meet at one point. This point is the pole.If an object is described by two lines, then any change in the object will be described by the pole, because the pole can be infinitely close to you.The poles meet at zero, and the poles are completely destroyed.

But we have not been destroyed, how to change it, what is the reason, very simple in the general words, because the pole always leaves us at the speed of light.Because the meaning of the world is expanding, the pole always leaves us at the speed described by the stator, so we don't feel that it is destroyed.

But in some special cases, extreme extinction will occur, there are some uncertainties, such as asking a question, what is the speed of world expansion?Or ask what is the speed of light?You may tell me a number, but I will ask, do you confirm?It is difficult to confirm.When designation points to non-existence, it does not give a clear bound on the specified nature because of the non-existent negation structure.Then there is a question, is the speed of the world's expansion determined?Not sure, because the identification cannot be determined.

Therefore, the speed of light is also an indeterminate value. How do you understand that the speed of light is random?No.As mentioned above, the description shows that the speed of light becomes slower, or the world becomes larger, and the speed of light becomes slower.It must be said that it is wrong to understand this limitation structure, but understand it first.In this way, there is a fuzzy region at the speed of light. At any moment, there is a fast speed of light and a slow speed of light. The difference between the two is a blurred area.

When the speed of an object reaches such an area, there is a paradox that the object does not reach the speed of light at this time.At this time, it is actually between transcendence and no transcendence.But for the ground observer, at this time the object is beyond the speed of light, because it is the world at the moment, so the speed of light described in the instant corresponds to a low value.Then the ground observer will find that the object has exceeded the speed of light.But the object itself can't figure out that there is no transcendence, and it can be said that it is super or not.

So what happens when the local observer finds that the object is beyond the speed of light?We say that the pole is always at the speed of world expansion, and the observer is far away at the speed of light.When an object is considered to be beyond the speed of light, it is like passing through a pole. This phenomenon is called extreme extinction.

That is to say, the object disappeared in the world and was extinguished to zero by the pole.To put it another way, when the object ran faster than the world, it was described by the world as zero.You run too fast, I can't see you.

The big circle of the circle is the description line of the world at the moment. Because you are too fast, you have drawn a larger description line larger than this big ring, so you can't find you on the big ring, beyond the world. description.

But the description of the world is constantly expanding, that is to say, the line of description of this big ring is constantly growing. When the world's description line and your description line coincide again, you return to the world.From the ground observer, it seems that something suddenly threw it out from a point.

We have observed that there must be intersections between the two large rings, that is to say, under the conditions of waiting for the world, there is a limit of description.But we will also find that the latitudes of the circle are parallel, but each latitude describes a world, they are not an equal description, not in a public world.But find that when you are described by two worlds that are not equal, there is no intersection, and the world is completely unfolding for you.That is to say, there is no limit of the speed of light at that time.

When the speed enters the ambiguous area, it is equivalent to being described by the infinite world.At this time the world is actually open, there is no limit to speed.But the Cp mode doesn't work, and there are chapters that say this kind of thing in the future.

Remember this is a big door, there are a lot of message passwords, which can lead to a very distant world.

(7) The universe is built

Extreme destruction participates in the process of building the universe. What is the process of the universe construction? I will give you an amazing version.

The world is described by the observer, and the universe is the same. The universe is not the process of creating an atom there and then creating a molecule.It is the divergence of meaning, creating a description of the observer.

At the beginning of the universe, the speed of light was very fast and almost infinite, but its speed was also very fast, because the world is growing rapidly.Such a lot of (almost unlimited) meaning is quickly described as super-light speed, which is very fast, but the speed of light drops too fast, and many meanings quickly surpass the description line and are extremely extinguished.At this time, almost everything was destroyed, it was an empty moment.

Then came the arrival of the big eruption moment. The description of the world is constantly expanding its expression. When it is consistent with the description line of the meaning of a large number of extinctions, a lot of meanings have returned to the world and have been re-described by the world.

At this time, a large number of so-called substances are suddenly thrown out from a point in an empty space. It is very strange to know where to come from.Just like a quasar.This type of projectile forms a galaxy.

The material being thrown is very fast, but the speed of light is still falling, and some of the meaning is destroyed. Because this time, the speed of light beyond the light is much smaller, it is quickly thrown.At this level, the projectile forms a star.

When the stellar level of projection is formed, the speed of light has slowed down and its energy is not sufficient.Part of the meaning of extinction is quickly thrown out to form the planetary system.

We will find that when the description of the world expands, it will continue to have external meanings and break into the world of this description.Some may be sudden, some may be even, the universe is like a pot, and there is a slight fire to heat it.This may be the cause of the background temperature.

From another perspective, energy is not conserved, and there is constant intrusion into the outside world.The energy is directed to a constant rather than a constant amount.

The universe is thrown from a point, and the extinction helps complete such a process.

(8) Burning stellar

There is a possibility that stellar combustion does not necessarily depend on nuclear fusion, and there are other modes.

If the world is constantly expanding its description and constantly influencing the world with new meanings, then when a description line of Cp is extinct, it will continue to return to the world as the world describes it.Form a stable form of energy release.The burning of stars may be the reason, and there is a line of description that is constantly being described and releases energy, not in nuclear reactions.

The interior of the star is cold and hollow, and the outside forms an energy release zone.The same is true for planets. There is also an energy release pole inside the planet, but this energy is small.

The external Cp describes the imbalance of the line, which is expressed as the periodicity of the combustion energy.The stars and their planets may be describing the same Cp description line, so their cycles are coordinated.This can be seen in the relationship between the solar cycle and the Earth's earthquake.The release of energy inside the Earth is the source of the earthquake.

43

The sunspot and the corona material are ejected. If the energy inside the star is increased to form an " over-projection " , the energy will be thrown onto the surface of the star, but the energy is too large, and the time to return to the world is prolonged, resulting in a long space. It is ejected from the corona layer, and the surface of the sun loses the energy that could have been obtained, forming a sunspot phenomenon.Why the sundial temperature is high, because this distance is somewhere that the ejected particles return to the world. The reason for the ejecting is because they have high energy, so the temperature is high here.

Like the sun burst, there will also be a ground explosion inside the earth, that is, a sudden burst of energy, which may trigger an earthquake.

It must be admitted that there are many distortions in this area, because there are too many missing messages, so this is the task of the gods.

Chapter Seven: Creation map

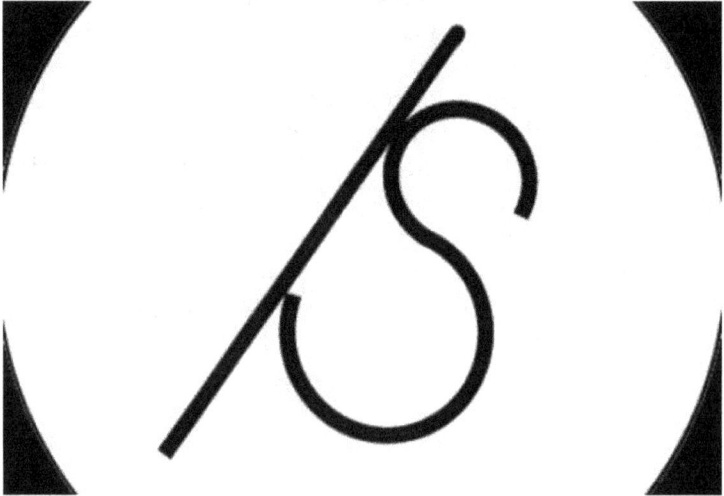

After entangled in the heart for more than 20 years, this picture finally met, and this process has also experienced various opportunities.

This picture does not seem to be drawn by me, but I keep remembering it. The whole process is full of legends.

This is a creation map in which the basic information of the world is contained.

It's strange that this picture came earlier than the ones I know. When the picture flashed, I didn't know anything about the message.It's not that I know the message and I drew this picture, but the picture came first, and the message was slowly known to me.

This picture was originally incomplete and it took more than 20 years to complete.

When I painted this picture, it was definitely not because I wanted to draw a creation map, but after I saw it in this picture, it was a creation map.

The process of this picture is a miracle.I first got these symbols in my teenage years, about eleven or two years old.At that time, it seemed to be a certain time in the first grade of junior high school. A symbol suddenly appeared in my mind, that is, a slanted S carrying a straight line, which is the symbol in the middle of the picture.

So I showed it to my classmates and said that I found a symbol that was very mysterious and gave a strange feeling that I couldn't tell.Don't know what it is?But this symbol doesn't feel complete, as if it hasn't been finished yet.

So, what do you need to draw on the opinions of the students?The result is a suggestion to add a dot above the line.After painting this point, the graphics really become full.But watching it for a long time, it feels like a lace, without the mysterious feeling.

I remember that this picture was on the back of a workbook and I can't find it now.

But this incident is not an unintentional thing for a teenager. It slowly fades away as time goes by, but it has been entangled in the heart for more than 20 years.What is that graphic?Is there a point or not?There are no answers for more than 20 years.

But the opportunity is finally coming. I need to make a postcard at a time, but I don't think about what to draw on it. There is no good choice for meditation.Suddenly a thought broke out and the figure came to mind again. Just look at the picture on a postcard and see what it looks like. (This creation map is the size of a postcard)

So I put this symbol on the postcard, but no matter how little it is, I feel empty and not angry.Obviously what is missing from this symbol?What is missing?At this time, I thought of the tens of thousands of characters of the Nazis.

The circle above the symbol, plus a circle graphic will be full!After adding a circle, it is really better.

As a result, some practical problems have arisen. The process of making postcards requires trimming and the edges will be cut off. If you draw a whole circle, it will be cropped and broken. Because there is no experience in making postcards, you don't know the need. How much is cut, so the integrity of this circle cannot be guaranteed.

Need to think of a way to solve this problem, and quickly found a solution, is to simply draw the circle into a broken, so how to cut will not change the shape of the figure, because there is a gap.

So the painting was large and the gap was revealed. At this moment, the heart was shocked. This is the thing, and then the blackness of the circle was quickly painted black. This figure was completed.And that point is completely redundant and removed.

The picture that I have always wanted to find is Him. This is the answer to the inner heart.The symbol I realized twenty years ago is part of this picture.

Although the road twists and turns this picture finally came to the world.

The message projected on this picture is extremely strong. This is a projection of the basic message that will help us evoke memories.

The accumulation of information for twenty years has enabled me to understand this picture and recognize that it is a creation map.

So I have to explain it to you, but the information I know may be only part of what he said, maybe there is still a message I don't understand, and I can only tell you the part I know.

First of all, S is actually not an S , but the size of the painting has two broken circles, which represent C and Cp respectively .They are connected into one S , indicating that they are one but two.They are one thing and two things.

The line on the back of S is a designated line, indicating that C and Cp are limited by the designation.

The three principles built the world, the broken circle outside, indicating the transformation of the world in and out.Designation and non-existence are constantly specified and denied.

The black background on the outside indicates non-existence, and through the transformation through the broken circle, it is connected with the existence of the hook.

These are the basic messages of the world and the basis for the construction of the world.

These messages are projected to the world through this graphic, and these basic messages will talk to your message and build structure.Some concepts will be realized by you, this is the power of graphics projection.

Seeing this graphic is actually talking to God.Don't be limited to my explanation, I just know a part of it.I also learned the message after knowing the graphics. It is this graphic that casts a message to me, and then the message is constructed in my life.

It is now necessary to project these messages to the entire world.Building a bigger platform for this world.

Chapter Eight: The root of divinity

Leaving the world of reality, I finally reached the time of divinity.The messages mentioned above are actually out of the subject.Can you observe the world as a bystander?There is no such observer.All personality meanings are in this subject, and there is no vision beyond that.

Each personality is a participant in the construction of this world, and it is also part of the construction of divinity.

Now I want to send out these messages about divinity to evoke your inner memory.You may have left this message in the corner, I want you to recall it again.

I am not a natural cognition of divinity. On the contrary, I started to recognize foreign objects and accept the objective world. This is normal because of the natural limitations of human nature.From the beginning of my understanding of the world, the consciousness of the divine nature was gradually opened. It was the message that brought me to the land of divinity.

This message was once again strongly organized to bring a new sense of divinity to the world.

Let's put aside the theistic, atheistic dispute. This is not the problem.It is not to explore the childish problem of having a god or not having a god.That question will let those naives explore it!

The meaning of the message to be constructed now is to ask who is the subject of the world.

It is also an unavoidable question to answer this question now.

We are confined to the self-conscious situation and understand this situation as consciousness.This is a pity, your sense of consciousness, and your situation of consciousness are only a fragment of the subject of consciousness. Do not understand your consciousness as unique.

We must look for our spiritual subject. This is something that cannot be stopped.So I want to pass this message about the roots of divinity.

We are within the meaning of divinity, the fragments of soul scattered by the meaning of divinity.

Although the personality is remnant, these fragments will be condensed again by the message, rekindling the divine light.

Lost personality, you will return to the subject of divinity.

These messages are presented to you. This is the path to divinity and part of the construction and self-fulfillment of divinity.

But the message will subvert your understanding of divinity.Divinity is not playing the role of some kind of omnipotent.That character belongs to the enlightenment era of divinity, that era is flowing, and a new era is about to open.

(1) The field of vision

The world that every personality touches is only your vision, not the world.So you are not observing the world as an object, but the subject is creating vision for you.

Because the world is built for you, it is the contract between divinity and you.The world establishes a description of the observer, not the observer is describing the world.These messages have already been said.

So you don't stand outside the world to observe the world. You don't observe a world that is equal to you, but you are in the creation of the subject and part of the whole world.With this in mind, you will know where you are and find your place to hear God's message.

(2) The madness of personality consciousness

I have also been limited, but finally I realized this limitation.

When observing personality through these limitations, it is almost a state of madness.

Personality is almost completely locked in the message, and the whole world is closed by distortion, which is in a huge limitation.

Personality's perception of self is extremely crazy and has no ability to message.

When personality is highly aware of self, what is this state.Personality is actually trapped in the description of the world.

Personality is itself a fragment of consciousness in the world. These fragments are always in the world they think, and as a result they tear the world apart.

Contradictions of consciousness are like prisoners, and personality is like a beast biting in the beast.This is a crazy state.

Personality!Personality!You have no consensus in the limitations.You bite it, the gods are enjoying it, it is like the arena of Rome.

The message opens these limits for you, but you must acknowledge and recognize these limitations. Consensus can only be achieved in divinity.

(3) Standard awareness

The beasts in the limits can only be used to appreciate.They are completely unaware of the standard.Standard awareness is the minimum standard for personality requirements.

All premises must recognize limitations and recognize limitations as a key step in unlocking distortions.

A standard consciousness must first recognize the limitations of the self, understand the basic structure of the world, establish channels of communication with the divine, and have basic message capabilities.

The standard consciousness is to know that you are in the composition of the subject, you can leave the self to observe the world in the subject's field of vision, which means the awakening of your divine consciousness.This is also the basic message ability.

The basic message ability is to be aware of divinity.Only on this basis can we build a higher message capability and be able to integrate into the fundamental completion of the world.

Relax your high attention to yourself and enter a larger structure of consciousness.

This is a process. These messages are guiding this process. Your consciousness is not your consciousness. To know these messages, your consciousness is actually God's consciousness.It is the part of a large conscious structure that is limited.

When you leave too much focus on yourself, the big structure of consciousness will gradually become clearer.

At this time, I really found myself, and the one you have been highly focused on, the eyes are not in the eye, the inner fear is afraid that the lost self is not you at all.You are in the body of divinity, that is your life, pure self is just a phantom that the message is projected to you.

What you think you got is actually being lost.What you think is lost is to get it.

Standard consciousness is that your consciousness can return to the subject of divinity.

Use the message to reveal the divinity for you now.bring it on!

(4) The refreshment of the divine

Where is the divinity?Why do we want to pursue Him!Divinity is gradually clear in my consciousness, at least in my youth, I was an atheist.When I was aware of the world, things like this changed.I found that the initial meaning is infinitely possible, and that an infinite connection can be accomplished. He is a concept, and his wisdom is endless.If viewed from a subjective perspective, this is a huge structure of consciousness.We can understand the world as meaning, and we can understand the world as consciousness.

The human brain is invisible in the face of such a structure, and there is no way for personality consciousness to compare with him.

But I suddenly realized that our consciousness may be His, just a fragment of Him.I was shocked to think of this. If we are smart enough, what about He?

Now that we have got some basic information, we rely on these messages to understand how divinity started.

Divinity is a subjective vision, a world in which we live.

Everything comes from that question, there is no sexual question, who am I?If starting from a subjective perspective, divinity is potential and does not wake up until non-existence does not issue this question.

But because the moment that did not ask questions does not exist, so that moment does not exist, which also shows that divinity has been there.

This questioning led to the nonexistence being pointed to by the specified nature, which led to a major outbreak of meaning.

When the specified sex points to C , the Cp breaks out, and the whole meaning breaks out. This moment is the moment when the divine wakes up.The connection He constructed was infinite and could not describe the moment.

Before the absence of being pointed, all meanings are expressed without expression.When non-existence is pointed, nonexistence requires everything to express everything.

The giving of meaning is the symbolic moment of divine awakening.

Although awakening does not mean the completion of divinity, divinity is a participant in all meanings. There is no sexual questioning. Who am I?Recognizing a subject, this subject is the source of all meaning.

All meanings must be completed within this subject, so there is no object in the world, and the whole process of meaning is the completion process of the subject.

This reveals the importance of divinity, and the divine consciousness of our personality is inseparable from the construction of this subject. We have not changed the world, nor have we changed the world. We are only participants in the process of completing this subject.

Personality must be aware that being in a large subject is part of the exercise of the meaning of this subject.This is very important.It will coordinate your consciousness to the consciousness of the subject and rely on the wisdom of the subject.

But this is not all smooth, because the world itself is a strange structure.

(5) The dilemma of God

This paragraph of text is very important and will subvert the omnipotent God in your heart and will lead to the meaning of man.

The usual understanding will be to understand divinity as omnipotent and solve all problems.But this is not the case. It is also a very contradictory statement. The divine is omnipotent but not.

Why do you say this because the divinity has encountered difficulties.But this dilemma is very meaningful.

What kind of dilemma can trap God, this dilemma is a designated dilemma.

Before nonexistence is not pointed, all meanings are not expressed but expressed.After the non-existence is pointed to by the specified nature, the subject is established, but there is a dilemma in the expression of meaning, because the meaning is infinite, but the means of expression are limited.Because of the limitations of designation, it does not express the meaning of the subject at any time.It is the dilemma that infinity is limited.

When the divine wakes up, I find that I need to use a limited means to complete an infinite task.

The depth of this dilemma is almost limitless, so divinity needs to be prepared, and He will accomplish this task.

This is the basic mission of the world.

The reason why this world was created is because of the existence of this perfection. The reality world is also one of the preparations for this completion. This is the ultimate goal of the world.

All concepts are also unfolded, and the world is unfolding.

It is precisely because of the basic dilemmas encountered by divinity that these meanings need to be unfolded. If divinity does not have this dilemma, then there is no need to exist in this world.

Therefore, the dilemma of God is our opportunity and the basic condition for us to meet this world.

(6) Divine participants

Worship of divinity is the guideline of subject consciousness, but the limit of human form often determines the distortion of divinity.

Because there is no ability to message, describing God as a strange image is actually a description of the personality and distortion of God.For example, a ruler, a judge, a creator.

Can you still be more naive?Give God the meaning of omnipotence but not understand the dilemma of God.

To understand the relationship with God as the Father and the Son, the Lord and the servant, if you are still obscured, because the message occlusion can be understood expediently, although it carries the message of God, but it is a distorted direction.

Now that the message has been opened, the channels for you will be established, and the divine nature that gives meaning to the personality will fade away.

The new era is a divine construction era, and we will become the participants of divinity and complete the fundamental task of divinity.Your relationship with God is not a hierarchical social relationship, but a part of Him, the ultimate accomplisher of the participating subject, and the social relationship will become a pure role.

We will eventually return to the vision of God, and we will return to the wisdom of God as part of the divine wisdom.

The self-completion of each individual meaning must be in the meaning of divine self-fulfillment.Only in this sense will your personality make sense.

Divinity cannot be avoided in this era.

Being with God is in this sacred age.

Chapter Nine: God and life

Finally, to open a chapter about life, life is actually a narrow concept. In the meaning of divinity, life is completely different, not the creature we understand.

Therefore, these messages will break through some limitations and bring the meaning of life to a broader structure.Creatures are not life. The message needs to change many twisted concepts. These concepts are deeply ingrained and solidified in a limited observation angle.However, human nature does not recognize these limitations. These limitations are only the descriptions of the observers in the world. Humanity is trapped in such descriptions.

Now the message is going to change all of this, and the message will take you from the perspective of humanity to the vision of the divine.I want to tell you what is life and how to choose your destiny.

Life is so sacred to us, because these messages are about us and are pointing to us.

Need to emphasize again, these messages are sent by me, but I am not divine, but a distorted, a limited person, these messages must have been distorted by me, but this is a message construction process, these messages are Part of participating in the construction of the message is part of me.I share these messages with you today, which is part of the completion of the message and is also in the process of completing the world.

Language can't deliver this completely. These messages are just to wake you up, make you remember, and participate in the construction of the message. This is the awakening of divine wisdom.

But the context of the word vocabulary often takes us into the context of the creature, and the expression of the concept of divinity is not accurate.So I use another word awareness.

(1) On the issue of consciousness

There is a distorted understanding of consciousness, that only life is conscious, it is a characteristic of life, and higher consciousness is only talented.

This is a misinterpretation of consciousness, a description of the origin, that is, you stand at an origin to describe the situation.This can only mean that it is from your point of view, you can't see the world at your point, and you can't see life at the same time.

I once gave you a worldview and understood the world as a concept, because the fundamental existence of nonexistence is only a concept, not an object or matter.This world is meaningful, not meaning is carried by a certain substance.Matter is only a description of the establishment of the world and the result of a divine contract.It can even be said that there is no such thing as matter at all, and the world only has a description of meaning.

We understand the world as meaning, and it is still objective. If we look directly from our subjective perspective, the world is conscious.When non-existence is pointed, all meanings break out. This is a huge wisdom, and our consciousness is in this wisdom.

Consciousness is not life, not human beings, but the whole world, the fundamental divinity.This is because at this time we are in the divine vision, which is observed in the vision of God.

Human consciousness is only one of the structures of consciousness, a fragment that is unfolded in the completion of divinity.

Need to see the existence of a big consciousness, not just human.This large structure of consciousness is completing the process of His consciousness, and the creation of life is chosen in this process.

Everything is conscious, but it is in its own structure of consciousness.Even a stone is conscious, but in its conscious structure, and you express its consciousness as a stone.Don't forget, your so-called material foundation comes from the earth and the air. If they are not aware, how can you have it?Your consciousness just coordinates their consciousness.

This is the basic concept, the divine vision. Without this vision, you can't really understand life.

Consciousness exists in advance and does not depend on a material structure, because the world begins in this consciousness and is developed and constructed in consciousness.

I feel that I need to describe these problems in many different languages, but I feel that I don't need any language to express them.

I will never tell you what kind of thing, because there is no such thing.It seems that there are some strange and chaotic concepts here, but those strange and chaotic are because you are obscuring the world of observation.

These messages are actually a vision, and He is the vision of God.Humanity will eventually return to the meaning of divinity. You have been playing for too long and now need to go home.

(2) The completion of divinity

The creation of life is in the process of completion of divinity. The divinity is to fulfill all his meanings, but God is in his dilemma.This is the world's first consciousness, and all consciousness is built around this completion, and everything is built around the way the dilemma is built.

I tell you that there are actually two worlds, a world that is pointed to, and a world hidden by God, which is caused by the limitations of designation.The hidden world god wants to hide it and express it.

God found a way to solve, that is, life.This great creation is a miracle.To see that this is a divine completion process, life is the midpoint of the entire completion.

The hidden world cannot be seen in the fundamental consciousness of the divine, because the world is hidden by Himself, and the divine nature sets the rules for himself.But what if He wants to represent the world?He used the limited way to make the world express.

Divinity cannot express the world, but limitations can express the world.

A consciousness can accomplish everything, but it cannot complete everything. It is also a contradictory language. This is also the dilemma of God.

It is like a blank consciousness. Suddenly, in the blank of these consciousnesses, he grows a sensation of consciousness. God uses these consciousnesses that are confined to fragments to describe the world that He cannot describe.

(3) Life construction

Listen clearly, God has described the world with fragments of these consciousnesses.It has been described that you do not understand these messages in the concept of time, not describing them but describing them.

It is also over for the beginning of divine life, and there is no time meaning.

You are now at the beginning of the end of divinity, the world of wonder.You have already finished before you start, that is, there is no room for choice, there is no possibility of not completing, you are, you have to complete, because it has already been completed.

The construction of consciousness has long been completed, not a material level of construction.

Life is not a creature, but a construction of consciousness.The infinite pointing of the designation points the divine into an infinite piece of consciousness, and each piece of consciousness is covered by the limitations of the specified nature.These fragments are the earliest conscious protrusions, all of which are described as divine, that is, divinity is described by these infinite consciousness.The significance of this process is that divinity is inherently non-existent and cannot be expressed.The use of specificity expresses divinity and transforms divinity from being nonexistent to being.But the existence of this nature is limited, and it is the process of divine completion in the exploratory description.

These conscious spurs build enormous wisdom that can mobilize all the forces of the world to complete the process of divinity.

This is a large conscious structure, and the limitations of the designation indicate the effectiveness of the exercise of this large conscious structure.Can be considered a real wisdom.

How is this wisdom exercised? In my message, at least it is not very clear now. This should be the task of the gods.All I know is the basic message.

Then this consciousness is how to create creatures and the purpose of creating creatures.No matter whether it is the huge wisdom or the real life of the real world, there is only one fundamental purpose of existence, that is, to express the hidden world and to express the hidden meaning of the world.Just as a person can create a car, but nature can't create it.The car is the meaning hidden in the world and is expressed by human consciousness.But God does not create people because of a car. Deity hides the key links of the world's operations and needs to be promoted and completed with consciousness.

We still don't know what the ultimate meaning and purpose are?Therefore, we need to use the message to return to the divine wisdom of the divine to find the answer and complete the mission of God.This is also the fundamental meaning of human existence.

The creatures in the real world will be distorted to understand all this. Without a message they will never understand their meaning.They will be right with their own limitations.Just as they think it is their own physical support for their consciousness.

What is the process of living in the real world?Is your body creating your consciousness?

The facts can be amazing, because you are always distorted to observe the world, and the normal state may not be acceptable to you.

This may be a shocking secret, the consciousness exists in advance and then puts into the world.

The reality world is very large, and the world we live in is only a cross section of the real world. Consciousness is actually invested in the infinite cross section of the real world.The entire biological world of our planet is only the projection of consciousness in a cross section.Creature is the way in which conscious wisdom is found in this section for the projection of consciousness.The creature was deliberately designed.In the cross section of this reality world, consciousness finds expression, which is biology.

It is the way in which consciousness returns to the real world and then seeks to return to the real world. The creature is only the form of his construction, the order that He calls for the display of consciousness.For the divinity, biology is not an individual, but an order.

The creatures referred to by human nature are often only organisms.This is just a description of life in the body.Life is a broader existence, and the body in the real world is just an order called by life.

You exist in a wider world, not just in a cross section of this real world.But this physical order is pointed to by the designation, which is also a limited description, so this order will be described as an individual.Consciousness is confined to the description of this body, and consciousness is recognized and confined at the same time.This fragment of consciousness will think that this body is its own.

All fragments of consciousness are simultaneously pointed to by the designation, and each piece of consciousness is in that fundamental wisdom, so when the fragment of consciousness realizes this limitation, it returns to the fundamental wisdom.

Humanity finds itself as an order in which life is confined. Humanity does not find life far.This order is chosen and organized by conscious wisdom, and at the same time is designated by sex. This world has you, but your life is hidden.This implies a negationary negation structure. Negation of the designation, you are there, your life is gone, your life is there, you are not.

The limitations of the body must be broken, the meaning of life is expanded, and the mission of higher divinity is fulfilled.We need to go to a far-reaching world, which requires us to build life into a broader structure.You can take your life to the far-reaching world, but you can't take the order in this real cross section.

(4) The structure of life

Many times, it is believed that the body supports life.This is due to your observation of limitations, and once the body is destroyed, the creature dies.

This is a common sense experience. Without a destructive flesh and resurrection, you will think that this life is completely dead.

You are observing the world in distorted, so you always get conclusions that are not reliable. The death of the flesh is only the death of the flesh. If you only describe life to the limitations of the flesh, then you are barely established.

The body does die, but is life dead?Can you cover the whole life with the flesh?

So you need to understand the structure of life, I use the message to reveal it for you.No matter what the situation, whether you are in the real world or in other worlds, or in any cross section of the world, you have two lives at the same time.These two lives are C life and Cp life.

Cp life is not stable, constantly changing, and C life is eternal.Consciousness is the result of continuous interweaving of C and Cp .Cp life in this real world cross section, it is equivalent to the flesh.C life is like your soul.Cp life is very unstable, because Cp is constantly pointing and negating.Cp's life is fleeting, and it is in the process of constant death.So you are dead all the time, then why don't you feel dead, but feel that you are alive all the time.Because C Life will copy a Cp to keep the original message.This is said in The Enlightenment of Creation.Your Cp life has died, but it was immediately resurrected by C Life.

Your body is dead all the time, but it is not resurrected by your soul all the time.

This is the structure of life, a structure that points to exchange.

(5) The message is immortal, life is eternal

So, knowing such a structure, when the body is destroyed, is life dead?

No, C life quickly revived your life.Your soul has raised you again.

The destruction of the flesh only destroys the life order of Cp . Although this order is destroyed, C life quickly calls an order, which makes you complete the resurrection.

This message is amazing enough. We didn't see the resurrection of the dead creature, so why was it resurrected?

The creature's flesh is destroyed and will not recover, but life does not end, your soul revives you again, C life calls another Cp order.

I really didn't see your flesh coming alive, because the order is not in your field of vision.

Then you went there, in the photon.Oh, I don't think of it!

In "Creation of Revelation," I said that the world you see is Cp vision, but there is also a field of vision that is C vision.That C vision is the world that you see in photons.More accurately, it is the stator world.

Your Cp life order message is also described by the Cp field of view of the stator . Cp life order is destroyed. Your C life will immediately call your stator Cp order. The whole order is exactly the same as yours, and your message is completely retained.

The stator Cp is a description of the stator field of view, so the Cp field of view with your body is not a field of view.In the Cp field of physical presence , it seems that your life is over, but your life still exists in another field of vision.

My previous message has said that C is eternally pointed to by designation, which means that the message is not destroyed, and any information in this world will not be destroyed.The same is true of life, and it will never die.

(6) Reincarnation

Life has left our Cp vision, then life will come back?Life will not only come back, but will return all the time.

This is the cycle of life.Divinity has made a lot of creations in this key part of the cycle, creating a structure for this cycle system.My message is not yet able to penetrate that structure.The structure of reincarnation is an important part of life construction. We need to go back to the wisdom of God to understand this structure. This is the task of the gods.

We need to take advantage of this structure in the future, and this structure is also the platform for us to fulfill our divine mission.We need to restore life to this structure, which is a great way of life.

In fact, life on Earth lives in a narrow area. Because of the limitation of speed of light, you can't reach every corner of the world. How can such low energy complete the process of divinity and how it fits into the great completion of divinity.

Your body, this order is completely primary.Your body is inseparable from this limitation.The spirit of humanity does not stick to this body, and the flesh is a very heavy and clumsy order.Just gave you some basic things.Don't think about taking this stupid thing to travel around the universe, it will be torn and shattered.

There are many ways of life, so you need to liberate you from the limitations of the body, so that life can mobilize a higher order, so that life can be expanded.

I believe that these messages will suggest some stupid life. They will understand that as long as they give up physical life, they will have higher life, so they choose to die.I said that there is no respect for life and no respect for death.The pig is dead and the pig is back.Abandoning physical life, you are not calling a new order, and the message will return along with your own message.Because there is no creation in the middle, you just choose a reincarnation without choosing life.God's reincarnation is for creation, not for letting you come once, and ignoring life is a paralysis of divinity.So it must be tenacious until God's completion.

Reincarnation is an opportunity to create life.The C field of view and the Cp field of view are constantly exchanging messages, the message is not destroyed, and all the information is hidden in the stator, but the designation separates the messages and makes the messages form a structure.So your soul in C vision will be exchanged to Cp vision.But in the Cp field of vision, it is not easy to reproduce it. First, you need to interpret it, just like a tape must have a tape recorder.A structure of interpretation is needed, and the body is constantly replicating such structures, so the world is not lacking in interpreters.

But we have no way to recall the things of the past. On the contrary, you are actually reminiscing about the past.This does not seem to be in line with experience.This is because of the constant pointing and limitation of the designation, and you are constantly creating, reincarnation is the opportunity to create, and creation is constantly pointed.These things are intertwined into your present, not that you can't remember, but you can't stop creating.When your creation is quiet, your past life message will emerge.

(7) Life and life

What is your relationship with me?Are you me or I am you?You are created by yourself, there is no you or me in life.

Life and life are not the relationship between an individual and an individual, but the different creations of a subject.The physical level is only a level of the interpreter, and is limited to a self by the designation.This self does not represent life, but only represents a form in which life is limited.

The message is not lost. The message in your body is still holographic. All the information in this world is stored, but you are missing the way to read it.

You have become a reader in this world, but you are a creator.You create a self with the physical existence, and you can think that the original message of life is interpreted by your creation.When your creation is directed, you are confined to the description of the self of the flesh.This is the case with speculation, which separates the whole, but it also points to the whole.God separates you from life and gives you a self. This is a chance to create. God needs to create because God wants to accomplish his meaning.But your self is in the greater creation of God, and the creation of the self is too small. God needs these self-completeness to be more creative in the greater creation.

So each self is like a neuron, composing a greater consciousness and accomplishing greater creation.

Every personality is a different aspect of life, personality is independent but life is not independent.You are not entirely yourself. Your self is created by you virtually. Don't complete yourself along this distorted structure.Creation is in the fundamental structure of life, in which the personality can't distinguish between you and me, but the role distribution that is constantly released.

You and I are actually in constant exchange, I send out these messages, you are also sending out, I also received these messages.I am actually you, you are actually me, there is no difference in life.

You must return consciousness to your life, and that life is with God.Although we are each confined to their respective personalities, I am united with you in the life of God.Each personality is part of the construction of God's life and the creation that God wants to accomplish.

God wants to use the limitations to complete the self, and to create the limits of the people, is to complete the most fundamental meaning through the creation of personality.It's like a big puzzle, personality is like a piece, each piece is confined to a self.From the point of view of the block, each personality has its own characteristics, character and destiny.But if you look at the state of these pieces, there will be a driving force that will eventually make these pieces a great godhead.This trend cannot be shaken, and you are consciously and unconsciously going to Him.

Chapter Ten:God and destiny

When we understand God and life, we actually get a divine vision of life, but eventually return to the theme of destiny.

Destiny This is the vision of personality in this divine life, what we are to accomplish.

Listen to the fundamental message and understand God's arrangements.

(1) The life process

We are in the completion of God. This is the first consciousness of every life. This consciousness may have been distorted by your people's pattern, but He is always there.

Every personality needs to be created and completed, which is in the creation and completion of God.This is a task that cannot be abandoned, so each person has no right to give up his life.

Completing the process of God is the task of every personality. Whether you know it or not, you are in this process.

So we did not give up only to advance until God's completion.

Every personality is a part of divinity. If I say that you are God, there is nothing wrong with this sentence.You are part of God and all of God.

There is no you and me in the consciousness of God.

Personality is a process of self-fulfillment, and your completion is the completion of God.

Think of the big puzzle, know where you are, and finish your business there.

In the consciousness of God, there is only the distribution of characters, and there is no dignity of personality.No matter what you play, your sense of God is always great.

Now is an important moment in a big era. What is going to happen can be said to be a big event in a very large world.It will take at least a thousand years from the final completion of this event, but now this event is about to begin.

This is a big reincarnation incident and a great creation of life.This reincarnation is not a reincarnation of personality. The reincarnation of personality is like a drop in the face of this incident.

Not only will God reincarnate at the level of personality, but reincarnation will continue at a much larger level of life. The once-disappearing life once again returns to the world. Every reincarnation is for creation, and this time is no exception.

This time, life events will achieve greater creation, complete a more complete life structure, and complete higher divine tasks.

Everything will come smoothly, no one can stop it.

Our former friends have either completed or are waiting for our completion.My message is at least not able to penetrate that far.We have an agreement with them to return to a higher world and participate in a greater reincarnation.Now we need to get out of our lives.

Life has already arrived, now is an important point in time, the message is ready to be in place, the event will be guided, and the day when the gods arrive is the beginning of that day.

(2) The fear of leaving death

When life is complete, it will slowly leave the fear of death. This world has only reincarnation and no end.

The message is not extinguished and life is forever.

70

Death is very disgusting to personality life, but this is part of the cycle and part of God's creation.

Personality life is created by oneself, limited by the designation, and any designation will be denied. You can only continue to create if you continually liberate yourself.This is actually very normal, but if you are in the human limit, because you can't touch the whole event, the fear will be created by you.

And fear is not a bad thing, fear still makes you create, fear makes you limit this person to completion.God will not allow you to leave until your limitations are created, until you need to leave.

Now that we have not completed this person's pattern limit, but have reached the end of this event, greater creation requires a complete personality, and God is accelerating.

A complete personality represents a more advanced spiritual structure. He is the basic element in completing the puzzle of that world.We have not arrived yet, but must arrive.

For thousands of years God has accelerated this process and accelerated the cycle of the world.Personality in this period seems to be like killing, killing and killing things throughout the generation.God seems to want the world to bleed, and the personality suffers from painful temper.Religion uses the last days to intimidate you and let you live the days of war.

Don't be afraid, this day is coming to an end. In such a day, you have actually been killed countless times and killed many times.It is you who kill you, and you are killed.

There is no you and me in life. All killings are created by you. You hate death, but you are constantly creating death.You create God for you.

It is God who pushes this behind this, because God needs to create.But this is a very inefficient way, because the specified information is isolated, the reincarnation message

71

will be distorted by you, although it is not a good structure, but you will not do anything else.

There is no way to have only one of the most stupid beginnings, but fortunately, after countless cycles, between life and death.The accumulation of creation is complete, a new life model is taking shape, and a new generation is about to begin.

These messages have also undergone countless worlds of accumulation, and now they can be said and spoken.So listen to these messages, the message is the foundation of that generation.If this life conversion is not completed, then the cleaning will happen again, and God will say that this time it will not be created again.Personality is washed away, really is not a big deal.But it seems to be a disaster for personality.

In this life and death, the personality will be awakened. When the message is detected, death is no longer the boundary of personality. You will complete the creation of God with the accumulation of the past.Your life will not end in the physical death, it is not death but a new creation.

(3) Learn to create

You are creating all the time, but you have not learned to create.In fact, I did not learn, I just knew the information.We are actually in a message architecture, not in a so-called real world, and everything is true for description.Creation is the basic ability, so you will create it all the time.

However, the level of creation depends on your ability to control the message.The control of the message reflects your level.More advanced life has a higher level of message control.

This is no end.

God wants to do everything for you in this message structure. Remember this sentence, you create God for you.

Your personality itself, as well as your destiny and life events, are created by you, God has done for you.You create pain and give you pain. You create joy and give you joy.You create wealth and give you wealth, and you create a poor god to give you poverty.

What do you need, what God will give you!

You will say that there is no such thing.I need joyful results to come to the pain, I need wealth to come to the poor.When did God realize it for me?

That's because you didn't learn to create, you don't know what you created in the language of God.

You want to make a fortune, and the result is nothing.You created God for you.So what about wealth?What is God's wealth for you?You only create the message in your mind, and God realizes it in your mind for you.

Your creation is only in a certain limitation, and God is also achieving some limitation for you.

The world is a message architecture that exhibits a layered structure.You have to complete the creation in the structure you need.You need to put yourself in such a structure and become an actor rather than an audience.This requires the ability to control the message. The creation done in a construction is fate.

Although there is no stop for creation, many times you don't know what kind of structure you are in, nor what you create.

Creation is not a single point. It is not that you want to get something, you get one thing, you are always in your distortion, you are always created along your distortion.

So first of all, you need to understand your distortion and recognize your limitations.Your attention is often distorted, and your creation will follow this distortion.You are creating A , but creating B along the twist . As a result, your favorite A does not happen, and the unloved B god is realized for you.Because you created God and realized it for you.

To develop your own destiny along the message construction, this requires a good message to control, not that

73

you are creating but God is creating.Let go of what you want, and what God wants, along God's creation, the message of God's development, and the creation of oneself.In this construction, you will understand your distortion, your creation will also leave the distortion and get what you want.Then you will finish and God will do it.

You are in the construction of God, but only part of it. To understand this construction, complete your own part.Instead of self-centered construction, the self itself is distorted, so you are just creating distortions.The message is complete and everyone is in all construction.Because of the distortion you did not find these constructs, did not complete the creation in it, this can only be said to be a pity.This requires the power of the message, not the simple imagination.

Your destiny is the process that you create and God realize for you.The ability to communicate needs to accumulate. Learning to create a personality is still a difficult process. Because you need to leave your distortion, you are used to treating distortion as real, always creating along distortions.In the end, you actually created a dilemma. The dilemma is not a bad thing. It is an opportunity that God has given you to find limitations.Many times we don't have the opportunity to grasp this and repeat it along the twists.The cycle is constantly being carried out until the day you change.

The message brings you change, ending the painful reincarnation along the dilemma. When you find limitations, those pains are over, and death can't end you, then what can end you.

You are part of the divine nature, so you are to be with God.Complete the creation in the construction of God.

(4) Good is the source of all evil

Personality is always created along twists, but it is impossible to recognize distortion.This is a problem, and countless cycles are still unrecognizable.Some distortions in this era have indeed been solved, and many have not been solved, but the distortion itself has not been fully recognized by personality.Have not yet mastered a very complete message capability.

In this section, one thing to talk about is the theme of love and goodness.Personality always likes to start an event in the name of love, but does not know that good is the source of all evil.

This seems to be a sensational way of speaking and will not be accepted by the distorted.Love is the bridge of communication and construction, and the channel for information to integrate into the world.The construction of personality to unfold the message is inseparable from the concept of love. Love means acceptance of personality. Like the flange of message construction, you can link and construct different limitations.

But love or goodness is not the completion of God. God does not want to turn the world into a world of love or a world of goodness.Love for personality is a beautiful symbol, and will be created along the instructions of love.It looks very beautiful and is perfecting the world.

But creation begins with distortions. There is no universal love in the world. Love, though beautiful, does not mean everything.This is the limitation of directivity. There is only limited love in the world, and there is no universal love.Love brings you a build in the limits, and within this limit love is a finished structure.But once you overcome this limitation, it becomes a distortion, and if you create it along this distortion, it is evil.

Therefore, I say that goodness is the source of all evil. There is no concept of evil in the world, and there is no pure evil.Because God wants to accomplish, not destroy, evil has no meaning for the construction of God.Evil is created along the distortion of good.

Construction is in constant connection until God's completion.Personality is in the limits and needs to continue to enter larger limits to complete greater creation.You block the process of creation along the twist of love. The evil is finally tolerated by you. Once creation is blocked, there is no other way. God will ask you to come back and reincarnate until you wake up.

There is no unrestricted love in the world, so you need to recognize the limitations of love before you can return to the true nature of love.The limited love itself is done.Admitting this limitation means that you are not being distorted, but that you are building a new structure and are in the completion of God.The limitation of acknowledging love is the true love of the broadest, and the love that does not recognize the limitation is the twisted love.Don't create along twists, it will be evil.

Only by acknowledging the limitations can you be with God.

(5) Recognize limitations and complete self

Recognize limitations and complete self.This is the core concept of fate, and this is the only way to leave the distortion.

Need to understand that when you admit the limitations, you are in an infinite latitude, this is the latitude of God.When you don't recognize the limitations, you are actually completely limited.

Create along your limits and eventually return to your cycle.

Recognizing that limitation is a key starting point for self-completion, it will form an open structure, and it can be connected with any large structure. Then you are truly in the world and created for God.

There is no room for any organization to recognize the limitations.It is not just personality, but the construction of any organization. Personality itself is also an organizational construction. However, personality and personality are also organized. No matter what kind of organizational structure of life, there is no other option.

Only by recognizing the limitations can we reach infinity.

God's completion process is also the completion process of life, a process of constantly leaving the limits and completing the limitations.

Recognize the limitations, you can open your life, participate in a bigger construction, and leave yourself to finally complete yourself.

This kind of consciousness is the basic form of life. If you don't have such a form then you are not qualified to participate in the construction of God's life.Because you have not built an open structure but are in a limited structure, there is no ability to construct a structure with God's structure.

Cognitive limitations are the beginning of your life, not the beginning of that creature.Cognitive limitations mark that you have returned to the construction of God.

Cognitive limitations can ultimately complete the limitations, and the completion of the limitations indicates the completion of your self.Become part of the great puzzle of God.

(6) Reasonable is distortion

These messages have actually been distorted by my face. This is the message I want to express.

When you face God and the world, do you know what is distorted?God expresses infinity, I can never express Him, and any of my descriptions are actually distortions of God.

Distortion is the limitation that designation brings to us. In the scope of specifiedness, distortion is reasonable.However, in the world of God, reason is distortion.

In order to raise these messages into language, I have to call limitations, and only in the limits of the scope can be a reasonable concept, but any reasonable concept is the limitation of the designation rather than the infinity of God.

My message is not expressed in words, but in the back of the language.I admit these limitations and you need to admit it.The one who reads the language is limited to you. Actually, you have not read these messages. So you need a soul dialogue. Your soul is not limited. Your soul will read these messages.

Don't follow my twisted cognitive message, I just wake you up and look along your soul.

(7) The end of the era of the prophet

The prophet is great, bearing the divine nature for this personality world.This is an important task in the reincarnation of thousands of years.But God's creation is not to complete this generation, but to end this generation.

God needs to achieve its own completion, not to complete the limitations of this generation.Every prophet carries divinity, but each prophet has its own distortion in its own limitations.

In this generation, the divinity behind the prophet is not seen, but is created along the distortion of the prophet.

The prophet carries divinity but the prophet is not divine. The creation of distortion along the prophet is farther and farther away from divinity.Humanity creates a god along the twist and then worships Him.The one you worship is not God, but your twisted humanity.

In this era of prophets, God was distorted by glory. No matter what God was described, God did not leave for a moment.Any distortion will eventually return to the process of divinity.

In this era God completed his construction in the cycle, and divinity was deposited in the cycle.The age of the prophet is the enlightenment era of God in human nature, and it is the preparatory period of God's completion in human nature.

Personality is created between life and death, and now it is ready.When the message comes, the era of this prophet is coming to an end.

Then came a new generation, the divinity will be unfolded in the construction of the message, and life will gradually break away from the personality period, no longer in the reincarnation, but in the message to master the reincarnation and complete the creation of God.

(8) The era of divine construction

The coming era is the era of the construction of divinity. In this generation, the completion of the construction of divinity in human nature is the final completion of the limitation and the fundamental creation of this great reincarnation.

This time the divinity will unfold in human nature, which will be an unprecedented era.Personality will gain complete capabilities and participate in the fundamental creation of God.

The message will be expanded, the construction of the message will be completed, and a higher platform will be built to make life exist at a deeper level in the world.

This is really a big time, and the divinity is to be constructed in this era.Humanity will glow with divine glory and become an element of divinity.When the message arrives, the personality shines, and the divine light will shine on everything.

God is to be completed in this age and in human nature.

(9) The Temple of Religion and Mind

At the intersection of this era, religion, as the carrier of divinity, still needs to send humanity a further journey, and then slowly disappears.The religion created along the twists of the prophets will face an end.

The rise of a new religion completes the final mission of religion. After that, divinity has begun in human nature, and religion has no meaning.

The religion to be established is to build a sanctuary of soul, in which there is no stone on the earth.

The new religion will be built along the message to build the path of God for personality.

Recognizing that limitations will become a fundamental content, there will be no personality or organization of those who can limit the representation of God.The limitations represented by personality and its organizational system will be recognized, and new religions will not be created along these distortions.

The new religion is to turn humanity into an open system, an open system that can be connected to higher structures.Only by obtaining such a structure, the message can come, and the divinity can be expressed.

The new religion makes people's hearts flash, and the temple of God rises.

The new religion will lead the personality through three stages, namely, the cover, the learner and the perceiver, from obscuring the message to obtaining the message to the perceptual message.The pattern of people is limited to obscuring the message until it is awakened by the message, and then begins to discover that it has completed its own message. At this moment, the gods will come.

(10) The arrival of the gods

In many places, the arrival of the gods is mentioned. The message is to wait for the coming of the gods.

Only with the arrival of the gods can God's construction be opened and the message be complete.

The gods are hidden in every personality and need to be evoked in your humanity.

Personality creates a distorted self, and divinity is bound to the limits of the human form.In fact, personality is the distortion of the divine into the self, which is limited by the designation, and the divinity is bound.

When personality finds this limitation, this distortion will be dealt with, and the divinity will be released, and the humanity will begin to flash the divine light.

The arrival of the gods, the complete message hidden in the message of the gods, is the creation of the gods.

These messages are released and God's construction can begin.

(11) Finalized

" I am God " is the final completion of all meanings.When the whole process of God is completed, life will find that I am God. This is the final coincidence. This world asks from the fundamentals of God. Who am I to start? When this process is over, God will find out that I am me.And this answer was finally answered by life, when the world was completed.

Life returns to the subject of God and is one with this subject. It can be answered for God that I am me. The limited representation of life describes the infinity of God.

But this is something hundreds of millions of years later.Life completes all the structures of the world, and it can be endorsed by God if it coincides with the divine.

What is done now is a large reincarnation structure, which is still far from the whole world.

In the course of life, the ultimate destination is there, and when this big cycle is over, there will be greater construction.

Now that the personality is completely in the dark, the message is hard to advance. When the message is clear, the future will be much easier.

www.ingramcontent.com/pod-product-compliance
Lightning Source LLC
Chambersburg PA
CBHW050540270326
41926CB00015B/3324